PERFECTIONISM

Brian L.

Living Solutions
P.O. Box 616, Cork, Ireland.

Tel: INT'L Code + 353 21 4314300
Fax: INT'L Code + 353 21 4961269

e-mail: livhaz@indigo.ie
Website: www.livingsolutions.ie

 HAZELDEN®

First published March, 1985.

ISBN: 0-89486-259-6

Printed in the United States of America.

It's great to be great, but it's greater to be human.
–Will Rogers

Editor's note: Quotations in the text are from *As Bill Sees It,
(selected writings of A.A.'s co-founder)*. Copyright 1967,
Alcoholics Anonymous World Services, New York, N.Y.

Introduction

Bill W., co-founder of Alcoholics Anonymous, once described alcoholics as "all or nothing" people. They felt compelled to be "right" in addition to having a compulsion to drink. Believing the alcoholic's central problem was "self-will run riot," Bill W. concluded, "First of all, we had to stop playing God." He saw his fellow alcoholics trying to overcome their sense of personal limitation by attempting to be perfect. This usually resulted in more problems because people can't will themselves to be perfect or hope to live up to perfect ideals.

Bill W. had discovered a basic fact — that by accepting our limitations as imperfect human beings, we can learn to accept not only ourselves, but other people as well. This acceptance is crucial in recovery from chemical dependency. We need to see ourselves as clearly as possible before we can start to recover, and we have to reach out to others for help. We can do neither if we insist on exerting our own will, finding our own way, and being perfect.

As perfectionistic people, we simply expect too much of ourselves and others. Our attitudes keep us from using recovery methods, including the Twelve Steps of Alcoholics Anonymous, which could lead us to a contented sobriety. People with perfectionistic values are true children of our individualistic society. They feel they must solve their problem of being chemically dependent by fighting it and trying to defeat it. But this problem will not be resolved through willpower or attempts to control ourselves or other people.

This effort to control dependency does not bring long-term recovery in most cases because we are acting as if the problem is only the use of drugs. The illness affects us emotionally, mentally, and spiritually. Unless we can accept the illness as a fact of life, our attitude will be ambivalent and recovery will be difficult, if not impossible. Once the facts are accepted, it is possible to change attitudes and behavior that were caused by the use of mood-altering drugs. If we believe we should be perfect, the temptation will be strong to control our situation through individual willpower, and we will not look outside ourselves for the help we need.

The Twelve Steps can be the basis for recovery from chemical dependency and from our perfectionistic habits. Although the Steps should be practiced as a whole, I would like to show how four of them are particularly important to the perfectionist and the chemically dependent person.

Step One asks us to admit we are limited human beings, and that our chemical use and character defects have made our lives unmanageable. This admission is the basis of the other Steps and is essential to our recovery.

Step Two describes the realization that we cannot handle the disease of chemical dependency by ourselves. If we could, dependency would not be a problem. Instead, we must look to a "Power greater than ourselves" for answers.

Step Three requires us to surrender our will and control to that greater Power, as we understand it. We must be willing not only to believe we have limitations, but also be willing to act on that belief when seeking help.

Step Eleven describes how we can grow spiritually. Our values have certainly been affected by our chemical use and we need to grow and strengthen ourselves in our relationship with a Higher Power. Steps One, Two, and Three describe a process of growth that starts within ourselves and radiates outward.

The remaining Steps, Four through Ten, and Twelve, lead us through an examination of our relationships with other people. Practicing these Steps is a way to identify our self-defeating attitudes and replace them with healthier ways of life. Although there is an emphasis on examining our character defects and making amends to those we have harmed, we should remember that this is also an opportunity to reach out and connect with others in a positive way. It is through interaction with others that we can put ourselves in perspective and come out of the isolation most dependent people experience.

"Every A.A. has been, in a sense, a prisoner. Each of us has walled himself out of society; each has known social stigma."

There are attitudes and character defects common to most dependent people. We suffer from egotism, dishonesty, power-seeking, and lack of self-esteem, to name a few. Perfectionism is related to many of these shortcomings and can be dealt with in the same way as the others. It may seem to us that accepting and surrendering to our limitations represents a defeat, but in the end it is the only way we will find recovery.

The Problem With Being Perfect

Perfectionists idealize themselves, the world, and the people in it. We set standards that are impossible to attain every time. Our failure to live up to these expectations causes negative feelings that damage self-esteem, stunt our emotional growth, and close us off from personal experiences and other people. We try to control people and events but are frustrated despite our best efforts because many things in life are beyond anyone's command.

There are voices all around us saying we should be as perfect as possible. Winning is everything: "Your brother did better than that." "Why don't you have a job like his?" "Nobody else needs as much help as you do." We forget it is impossible to always please others, and we begin to think less of ourselves when we fail. We may not even be able to see how our expectations have made our lives unmanageable.

As perfectionists, we often consider ourselves worthless when we don't achieve our goals. Anxiety and depression result from the low self-esteem we feel after a personal defeat. It's easy to be frustrated and angry when we think life is not going as it should. Self-criticism is inevitable when we feel we must constantly succeed in order to prove our worth as individuals. We focus so strongly on self-criticism that we cannot admit our successes. We become disillusioned when our self-worth is tied to a losing struggle to meet an unattainable ideal. And we withdraw from life because we cannot find any guarantee of success.

This withdrawal is often caused by fear of failure. We refrain from activities if there's a chance we may not succeed. We are unwilling to take risks for fear of making mistakes. By doing only familiar things and not making new discoveries, we narrow our world and become bored. This withdrawal and self-concern keeps us from changing and growing even when we clearly need to do so.

Do we avoid conversations at work or in social situations because we are afraid of being considered ignorant? Do we refuse to participate in sports or other activities because others may see us as clumsy? Are we so rigid in our likes and dislikes that we're not open to listening to new kinds of music, reading books outside our interest, or eating unfamiliar types of food because we *might* not like them? People come to know and appreciate us through sharing experiences. If we stay in a small, safe world we only cut ourselves off from others and from the growth we could gain from new experiences.

The habit of procrastination is another form of our fear of failure. If we think we must perform our tasks perfectly, all too often we put off even trying. When we attempt to do everything as thoroughly as possible, nothing gets done because we build the task up in our minds to the point that it appears impossible. A too-casual approach can also be procrastination; if we only go through the motions in order to avoid failure we make ourselves unhappy with our performance.

Not really trying to accomplish something because we're already convinced we will fail reflects our low self-esteem. Many of us work as salespeople in that we need to convince others to buy a product or service, or accept an idea. Whether we are selling merchandise or presenting suggestions to our employer, we need to be able to risk failure. We get better by trying, even though we don't *always* succeed. If we don't really try to convince customers a product is good, or try to show why our idea is better, we end up behind our salescounters or desks going through the motions of working, using the minimum amount of effort. This damages our self-respect further because we don't feel we are making a contribution or that our work is meaningful. Putting off trying because we think things will somehow magically get better is just an excuse for doing nothing.

"Too much of my life has been spent in dwelling upon the faults of others. This is a most subtle and perverse form of self-satisfaction, which permits us to remain comfortably unaware of our own defects. Too often we are heard to say, 'If it weren't for him (or her), how happy I'd be!' "

When we take ourselves too seriously, self-criticism, low self-esteem, excessive pride, and fear of failure come into play. When our egos and sense of self-importance become too large, they keep us from seeing ourselves as we really are. We forget we are powerless over our shortcomings as well as our chemicals. And how we feel about ourselves relates to our use of mood-altering chemicals. If we feel inadequate and fail to win approval from others, do we look for comfort and feelings of self-worth in drugs? Do we think we must deny and hide any weakness because we are better than others and should appear unflawed? And when we do perform less than perfectly, do we blame it on others and relieve our frustrations with chemicals? Thoughts like "No one will like me; I won't fit in if I don't drink" or "My kids make me lose my temper when they disobey me. I need a drink to calm down" are ways to avoid facing reality instead of finding solutions to our problems.

These types of behavior are self-defeating and prevent us from enjoying life. We cannot relax if we are constantly demanding too much of ourselves, if our emotions are out of control, if we are unhappy because our reach exceeds our grasp. These are all ways in which our lives have become unmanageable. And most important, these attitudes keep us from experiencing the growth we need in our recovery. Recognizing our character defects for what they are is a beginning, but we need to be willing to find new ways of thinking and feeling if we are to grow and change.

Personal Growth

"Such is the paradox of A.A. regeneration: strength arising out of complete defeat and weakness, the loss of one's old life as a condition for finding a new one."

Personal growth requires the ability to change, and change will not occur if we continue to hold on to our old habits and ways of thinking. To admit we were not always right in the past and to acknowledge we are imperfect human beings is not a defeat, it is a mature and responsible action that prepares us for the changes ahead. Being open to new experiences will help in understanding and communicating with others who can support us in finding new identities.

"Adversity gives us more opportunity to grow than does comfort or success."

Life should not be something to endure or master. It is not always as good to us as we would like, but we can learn from our failures and pain. What seem to be serious setbacks can serve to remind us of our human limitations; they will be blessings if we gain from them some amount of humility, honesty, maturity, or balance in our relationships with others. These are qualities we need to cultivate in our lives in order to grow and change for the better.

Humility comes from placing ourselves in a proper perspective and being willing to face facts. We gain freedom from false pride and arrogance when we find a realistic relationship with other people. If we can see we are no more important than other people, no better or worse, this realization will help us find our proper roles in life. We can rejoin the human race in a spirit of cooperation and show genuine interest in people and things outside ourselves.

Honesty is required if we want fairness in our relationships. If we sincerely desire to work at our recovery, we should be willing to admit when we are wrong and be candid in detailing our character defects.

"To those who have made progress in A.A., humility amounts to a clear recognition of what and who we really are, followed by a sincere attempt to become what we could be."

Practicing humility and honesty in our lives will help us reach the maturity needed by all chemically dependent people. When we stop overreacting to insignificant problems and start acting in a self-respecting manner, we achieve balance in our lives. Arguing about insignificant things is a symptom of always having to be right. By being more patient and understanding we curb our impulsive habits: "If you can't get it for me now, please do it as soon as possible," or "I can understand how you feel, but please consider my viewpoint as well."

Honestly sharing our thoughts and feelings shows willingness to do without the defenses and masks we hide behind: "That hurts my feelings, and I'd rather let you know how I feel instead of finding ways to hurt you," or "I really appreciate your offer to help, but I need to do this myself."

If we are willing to rid ourselves of our limiting character defects and work towards becoming better, happier people, we can find a positive approach to life. It means developing a new feeling of self-worth and self-respect to replace the self-serving habits that stunted our growth. Self-centeredness also kept us from having good relationships with others — those who could help us find a new way of living.

Reaching Out To Others

The qualities of honesty, humility, and maturity are as important in our relationships with others as they are to us. Our self-image and self-expectations control our feelings about other people and our actions toward them. The self-defeating behavior that limits our potential to improve our personalities also damages the way we relate to those around us.

If our expectations of ourselves are unrealistically high, we will be intolerant of other people's abilities. They will rarely be able to meet our standards or do things as we think they should. As long as we feel we are always right, no other opinion or method will appear as good. It's difficult to maintain friendships if we constantly find fault, and we will not be respected if we set ourselves up as judges.

Because of our compulsion to control ourselves and others, we may try to improve people. Manipulating their lives and trying to fix their problems gives us the illusion of power we need to feed our sense of self-importance. Some examples are domineering spouses ("I *told* you not to do that, but you never listen to my advice"); overprotective parents ("You can get hurt playing ball, and you always come home dirty"); or demanding employers ("We expect all our employees to take work home").

If we assume responsibility for our actions we can even convince ourselves we are *acting* responsibly, rather than simply exercising our egos. At times we do need to give advice, but it would be wise to ask ourselves if we are sincerely trying to help the other person rather than trying to control him or her for our own purposes. Do we really have *their* best interests at heart, and are we really able to take responsibility for the effect we may have on their lives?

9

Setting arbitrary standards or expectations for individuals or groups of people not only allows us to play God, but robs others of their right to be different. While placing too high an expectation on people can be unfair, it is equally damaging to expect too little simply because these expectations are based on our narrow prejudices rather than on an individual's actual abilities or character. If we are fair in our expectations and show honest concern for others, we will allow them to develop to their fullest potential in all areas of their lives.

Perfectionists are particularly prone to emotions like jealousy and resentment because we feel we deserve many things we cannot have. Jealousy is the fear of losing something we feel belongs to us. We don't own people, for example. Jealousy does not result from loving another person; it means we resent not being able to own or dictate other people's feelings and actions. These negative emotions not only harm our relationships, but are also dangerous to our sobriety if they become excuses to use drugs.

Our perfectionistic habits have a negative impact on our ability to get along with others. And worse, eventually we shut ourselves off and try to live in a world constructed by and for ourselves. We know from our A.A. experience that there is a Power greater than ourselves that can help us if we look beyond ourselves to find it. This is only possible if we open our lives to others and ask for help when we need it.

"Our very first problem is to accept our present circumstances as they are, ourselves as we are, and the people about us as they are. This is to adopt a realistic humility without which no genuine advance can even begin."

Accepting the imperfections of other people can help us accept our own limitations. An attitude of "live and let live" will be more beneficial than adopting a critical attitude. Putting ourselves in another person's place can help us understand their problems and motives. This helps us keep our lives in perspective and practice humility.

Drawing people into our lives will be difficult if we act as if we are perfect and don't need friends. We can make ourselves accessible by not denying or hiding our imperfections. Others will identify with us more easily if we appear humanly fallible, and by sharing our fears and doubts with them, we realize it is acceptable to be human. For example, parents should not be afraid to admit their mistakes: "It was wrong for me to have lost my temper when you tore your clothes playing, and I'm sorry. I know you didn't do it on purpose. I just worry that you could get hurt."

Many people feel guilty about their limitations and shortcomings. We can help them accept themselves if we are willing to share our experiences and offer understanding and support. As recovering people, we may particularly regret our past drug-related behavior. We can help ourselves by reaching out to others and finding a common bond.

Avoiding Perfectionism

"We demanded more than our share of security, prestige, and romance. When we seemed to be succeeding, we drank to dream still greater dreams. When we were frustrated, even in part, we drank for oblivion."

If we truly want to feel better about ourselves and live happier lives, we can find new ways of thinking and acting which will relieve the pressures we feel in many areas of our lives. If we believe we need to change, our belief will form the basis for our actions. In order to change our attitudes we need to convince ourselves that adopting a different perspective on life will be helpful.

Our perceptions of people and our reactions to events have been inappropriate because they have been extreme. Our expectations about the outcome of events and how we perceive the actions of others upset us more than the events or people themselves. We are in the habit of *awfulizing:* "It's just awful that the car broke down!" Events are seldom as bad as they seem. It is our interpretation of their significance that can be upsetting. If we choose to regard every situation, no matter how insignificant, as a disaster, we will never find any peace of mind. It would be better to say to ourselves, "It's inconvenient that the car broke down, but at least it can be fixed," or, "I wish I were on time, but being late doesn't mean I'm a worthless person or that my life will be ruined." We should not use this approach to excuse or rationalize; we still need to face facts and accept the consequences of our actions. But categorizing events in absolute terms is absurd. Keeping our lives in perspective and avoiding the habit of magnifying events out of proportion can prevent a lot of unnecessary anguish.

We have assumed that if we can act as perfectly as possible others will admire and love us. We try to gain and keep that respect by thinking in absolute terms: "I *must not* make a mistake that will embarrass me." "I *should* perform well or my friends will not like me." Thinking in terms of "shoulds" or "musts" puts a heavy burden on us and only makes us miserable when we fail. If we realize that, however desirable our goals may be, we don't *have* to accomplish them, we will discover we are more content.

Our worth as individuals is not measured by the perfection of our actions. We all have strengths and weaknesses and varying abilities. We may fail at something, but that alone does not mean we are bad people or that we cannot succeed at another time or in a different situation. Even when our actions seem perfect we would be wise to remember that we remain imperfect human beings.

Perfection is a subjective, abstract ideal few people agree on. We can certainly take pleasure in our accomplishments that seem perfect, but it would be foolish to expect that kind of success all the time. If we impatiently pursue abstractions such as perfection and happiness in our lives, we probably will be too distracted to enjoy the smaller pleasures and satisfactions that come our way. If we are living for today, we will take the time to find and appreciate experiences that give our lives more joy and meaning than any perfect achievements could give us. It is helpful to remember that only we can measure our happiness or success. Allowing others to judge it for us means we would be trying to conform to their idea of what is right for us.

"We neither ran nor fought. But accept we did. And then we began to be free."

We progress when we try to be better, not when we try to be perfect. Growth usually happens in small stages over a period of time. By setting more modest goals and lowering our standards, we will feel better about our abilities and perform more efficiently. Working at a level where we can be successful is much more productive than pushing ourselves toward goals we cannot reach. Our successes will bring satisfaction in a job well done instead of the tension and anxiety of constantly trying to perform beyond the limit of our capabilities.

Identifying the things we do well helps maintain balance in our attitudes. But we also need to accept the fact that we will make mistakes and can learn from them. We may not find out what we need to know *unless* we allow ourselves to make mistakes, so we might as well accept it as a learning experience and get what we can out of it.

Perfectionists are people with lives rich in achievement but poor in joy. If we stop to consider our accomplishments, we may see that we have been successful in spite of our perfectionism rather than because of it. Happiness and success should be a way of life, not a goal.

If we can surrender our will, admit that we need help, and reach out to others, it is possible to make the changes we need and experience the growth that can help us become happy, whole people. Being imperfect gives us opportunities to learn, meet challenges, become better people, and take satisfaction in our improvement.

Alcoholics Anonymous' Twelve Steps to recovery are as follows:
1. We admitted we were powerless over alcohol — that our lives had become unmanageable.
2. Came to believe that a Power greater that ourselves could restore us to sanity.
3. Made a decision to turn our will and our lives over to the care of God *as we understood Him.*
4. Made a searching and fearless moral inventory of ourselves.
5. Admitted to God, to ourselves, and to another human being the exact nature of our wrongs.
6. Were entirely ready to have God remove all these defects of character.
7. Humbly asked Him to remove our shortcomings.
8. Made a list of all persons we had harmed, and became willing to make amends to them all.
9. Made direct amends to such people wherever possible, except when to do so would injure them or others.
10. Continued to take personal inventory and when we were wrong promptly admitted it.
11. Sought through prayer and meditation to improve our conscious contact with God *as we understood Him,* praying only for knowledge of His will for us and the power to carry that out.
12. Having had a spiritual awakening as the result of these Steps, we tried to carry this message to alcoholics, and to practice these principles in all our affairs.*

---

*Alcoholics Anonymous, published by A.A. World Services, New York, NY, pp. 59-60. Reprinted with permission.

Other titles that will interest you . . .

Perfectionism
From Hazelden's Rational-Emotive Behavior Therapy Program

Use this pamphlet and workbook to help you positively respond to your perfectionism. Realistic situations and lighthearted illustrations, combined with open-ended questions and other exercises, will guide you to a new understanding of the 11 most common perfectionistic traits—and your power to change how you react.

Perfectionism   22 pp. pamphlet   Order No. 2882
Perfectionism   15 pp. workbook   Order No. 2891

Passages Through Recovery, Revised
An Action Plan for Preventing Relapse
by Terence T. Gorski

Stay firmly on the path to recovery. Terence Gorski, an acknowledged recovery expert, highlights the "stuck points"—including character defects and troublesome situations—that can lead to relapse. An excellent "plan ahead" guide. (155 pp.)
Order No. 5687

Letting Go of Shame
Understanding How Shame Affects Your Life
by Ronald Potter-Efron and Patricia Potter-Efron

Build your self-esteem and find out what effects shame can have on your self-image and your relationships with this intriguing book. Exercises, personalized plans of action, and simple outlines all help you get in touch with your feelings of shame. (192 pp.)
Order No. 5082

For price and order information, or a free catalog, please call our Telephone Representatives.

◪ HAZELDEN®

Living Solutions
Pleasant Valley Roa~~~~ P.O. Box 616, Cork, Ireland. ~~~~enter City, MN 55012-0176

Tel: INT'L Code + 353 21 4314300
1-800-328-009{ Fax: INT'L Code + 353 21 4961269 ~~~~nada & the Virgin Islands)
e-mail: livhaz@indigo.ie
1-651-213-4000 (Website: www.livingsolutions.ie & Canada)
1-651-257-1331 (24-Hour FAX)
http://www.hazelden.org

ISBN 0-89486-259-6

Order No. 1404

9 780894 862595   90000